101 WAYS TO SPOIL
YOUR HUSBAND

by Tena Brown

Honor Books
Tulsa, Oklahoma

101 Ways to Spoil Your Husband
ISBN 1-56292-813-9
Copyright © 2001 by Tena Brown

Published by Honor Books
P.O. Box 55388
Tulsa, Oklahoma 74155

Printed in Canada

INTRODUCTION

Men are so simple! I have a very special affinity for men because I had such a wonderful relationship with my dad. He adored me, and I adored him. I have found such joy in delighting the men in my life and look for ways to show my love and gratitude.

It takes only a little effort to keep them happy. It surprises me to hear how unhappy some husbands are. My mother always taught me that men were simple and thank goodness for that. God made them that way since women were so *complicated!* She always said you can make a man follow you to the ends of the earth if you will just do these simple things on a regular basis.

—Tena Brown

MOM'S RECIPE

1. Make him lots of homemade chocolate chip cookies.
2. Scratch his back and rub his feet.
3. Give him lots of intimate pleasure.
4. Offer him meaningful conversation—stimulate his mind.

It is my most sincere desire to help women find ways to love and adore the men in their lives. Why? Because it's so much fun, it makes you feel good about yourself, and it creates fertile ground for your man to become all he is meant to be. Behind every successful man stands a woman. I believe we women have —and always have had—the power to truly help our men and to encourage and love them into becoming strong and powerful leaders. *Make him a king, and he will make you a queen.*

It's time to start loving our husbands—teaching, nurturing, and truly being their best friend. There are occasions when you have to help correct and instruct your hubby. This must be done in a loving way, showing him how to get back on the "right track" and gently nudging him there. I believe this is the way God intended us to be.

If your marriage needs a spark or you have long dreamed of having a "match made in Heaven," then start now and make it happen each day. Your husband will thank you and follow you to the ends of the earth!

—Tena Brown

1.

ONE

Constantly remind him of all the
reasons you married him. List them for him,
and tell him these things as often as you can.

You might even recall a few things you had forgotten about! I
make a regular habit of telling my husband, Ron, why I married
him. I also remind him of promises he made before we got married
that I expect him to keep. It really is good to remember the reasons
you fell in love, and since you've been married, maybe he has given
you even more reasons to be in love with him. Remind him of
those things, too.

2.
TWO

If your husband likes sports, (and what husband doesn't?) go to a football, baseball, basketball, or hockey game with him sometime.

3.
THREE

Bring him his favorite hot beverage in the morning to help wake him. It helps set a tone for the day. It's the simple little things that warm his heart.

4.
FOUR

Give your husband a back rub, foot massage,
or scratch his head and watch him purr. They
absolutely love this stuff, even if they won't tell you.

Serve wholeheartedly, as if you were serving the Lord, not men.
Ephesians 6:7 NIV

I hear a lot of women say, "I'm not going to do this or that for him," and "I'm not his servant." My philosophy is when you do these things, you minister to him. You are telling him with your actions how much you love him, and you are being a servant. We are called to be servants and to love our husbands.

5.
FIVE

Go out and wash the car with him once in a while.
It's not that he really needs your help,
but he just might need the company.

6.
SIX

If you have access to a computer, e-mail him
a special love message. It's the element of
surprise that will make him smile when he
receives it, and it reinforces your love for him.

7.
SEVEN

Start the shower for him in the morning.
(Sometimes he will need your help
just finding the shower.)

Once again, this is simple. We all know he can turn on his own shower, but it could start the morning off right when you've done something so simple as to let him sleep an extra minute or so while you get the shower hot. These thoughtful little things are missing in so many marriages.

8.
EIGHT

Always be affectionate. A gentle touch, a hug, a kiss on the cheek. Most men act like they don't like this or need it. But trust me, they *love* it. This is one of those things that sends a signal to his heart and soul.

Greet one another with a holy kiss.
Romans 16:16 NIV

I believe simple affection is a key ingredient so often left out. We must continue to reinforce an attitude that shows we love him even in the small, simple gestures.

9.
NINE

Don't whine about things.
Develop an attitude of gratitude.

*Better to live on a corner of the roof than
share a house with a quarrelsome wife.*
Proverbs 21:9 NIV

Men hate whining. It's like an annoying, dripping faucet. Be thankful, grateful, appreciative, and learn to take things lightly. I have been around so many women who whine about every little thing. Then they wonder why their husbands don't want to take them anywhere or be around them. This is such a big *don't*. Ron never hears me whine about anything. Whining will only drive him away.

10.

TEN

If he is out working in the yard on a hot day, bring him some iced tea or another cold beverage. This says to him that you care, you notice what he is doing, and you appreciate it.

Let us not be weary in well doing: for in due season we shall reap, if we faint not.
Galatians 6:9

Ron loves iced tea, so every Saturday morning one of the first things I do is make him a pitcher of tea. He loves knowing that I am taking care of him. He works hard in the yard and keeps the cars clean, so the least I can do is keep his tea glass full. Try this! Let your husband see that you are looking after him. It sends a strong message of appreciation to him.

11.
ELEVEN

When he least expects it, make reservations
somewhere and take him out to dinner.
You make all the plans.

12.
TWELVE

Let him sleep in some Saturday,
while you get the housework started.

Hint: Postpone the vacuuming until he finally awakens.

13.

THRITEEN

Go shopping for him one day.

Don't take him with you—just surprise

him with something you bought him.

This is fun—and easy. I love for my husband to smell good,
so often times when I am out, I buy him a new bottle of cologne.
Sometimes I find a shirt that I would like to see him wear.

14.
FOURTEEN

Call him at work one day just
to tell him you are nuts about him.

Hint: Don't tell him you're nuts *because* of him.

The entrance of thy words giveth light;
it giveth understanding unto the simple.
Psalm 119:130

15.
FIFTEEN

Do romantic things often. Give him
those starry-eyed stares, send him candy,
buy a romantic new CD for quiet times alone,
dress the way *he* likes you to around the house.

All of our men differ in some way, but *you* know what it is that
romances your husband. Do it often. Don't let life get so hectic that
you don't make time for romance. Staying in love and doing the
things that caused you to fall in love in the first place give you an
escape to where you really want to be.

17

16.

SIXTEEN

Tell your husband daily how much you
love him. Men need this constant reminder.
This continues to reassure him of your undying
love, giving him, one less thing he has to worry about.

17.

SEVENTEEN

Make sure you hold hands when in public.
It should always be obvious that you are in love.
This sends a strong message to others—
including your children—and it makes
you feel good about each other.

18.

EIGHTEEN

When eating out, do simple things
like sweetening his iced tea or unfolding
his napkin. This is a simple servant attitude.

This is a given for us. When Ron orders tea at a restaurant, I always sweeten it for him. I love to do this. Too many women look at this as lowering themselves to a servant status. You know what? I am in love with my husband, and I like to show it in simple things. My husband will follow me to the ends of the earth. He knows he couldn't replace me. I love knowing that I've captured him in every way. You can do the same.

19

19.
NINETEEN

Bake him cookies. Always keep a fresh batch of chocolate chip cookie dough (or whatever his favorite is) ready. This will tame the cookie monster in him. Men *love* sweet treats.

Hint: Try not to eat all of the dough while you are making cookies, or you'll totally defeat the purpose.

This is probably my signature act. I make chocolate chip cookies every week—literally. Ron loves them, and so do all the friends and neighbors. I usually make cookies for our local mechanic Gus, our video guy AJ, and plenty of other friends. My cookies have cured many late-night hunger attacks for Ron.

20.
TWENTY

When he is half dead from performing a lot of chores, run him a hot bath and wash his back. Sit with him and just be his best friend.

A friend loveth at all times.
Proverbs 17:17

21.

TWENTY-ONE

Commit yourself to learning, growing, and filling your mind with valuable, worthy things. Be the kind of wife that would make any husband proud. Every man loves to talk to an interesting woman.

The most powerful, sensual organ you have is between your two ears. We will never know all we should, and we can improve our minds. I want to always be interesting and informed. Your husband will never be embarrassed when you can carry on an intelligent conversation with his friends, his boss, his parents, etc.

22.
TWENTY-TWO

Do things with him that interest him.
Show enthusiasm for his hobbies, crafts, or special-
interest projects that he gets involved in.

My husband loves cars and motorcycles. I have gone to swap meets with him, looking at old cars and parts. It means a lot to him that I show interest in his world. I can't tell you how many cars and motorbikes I've seen, but it's an excellent way I can show him that his interests are worth my time. Learn to show interest in his likes.

23.

TWENTY-THREE

Surprise him with a special gift—
for no special reason.

Think of something your husband has been really wanting but never purchased. Wait 'til you see his face light up when you walk in with a special gift for him. I have seen things too many times that I know Ron would like. My problem is that I can't afford them all. But it's the thought that counts, and it's fun to buy things for him.

24.
TWENTY-FOUR

If there are any "broken fences" within
the family, do your part to help mend them
as soon as possible. There is more value
in this than you could ever imagine.

A soft answer turneth away wrath:
but grievous words stir up anger.
Proverbs 15:1

25.

TWENTY-FIVE

Learn all you can about being a smart wife—
the kind of woman that will keep your husband
interested. Remember, men are hunters and
gatherers. Give him something to hunt!

(This doesn't mean you should wear the bear
rug, although that could be interesting.)

26.
TWENTY-SIX

If your husband has an ex-wife, be kind and loving to help matters in every way. Even if she doesn't respond favorably, it will remind your husband that he made the right decision in marrying you.

A new commandment I give unto you, That ye love one another.
John 13:34

You can live in misery and always be upset, or you can try to get along and do the right thing. We may never do things perfectly, but we can control how we act and react. My civility in these matters really makes my husband feel he can trust me. It's never the best situation, but *you* can make it as good as you choose.

27.
TWENTY-SEVEN

Make a habit of writing and leaving him fun love
notes. You can leave them on his pillow, on the
bathroom mirror, in his car, etc. These simple acts
of love help to keep him falling in love with you.

Do you realize how much it would mean to your husband if
you would surprise him with a card or love note? I leave them in
different places—the bedroom, bathroom, or in his closet. I know
it helps him feel secure with my love. I also leave them in his car so
he can find them on the way to work.

28.
TWENTY-EIGHT

Exercise!!!!! Every man wants his wife to keep her girlish figure, so do everything you can to keep yours.

Some of you were blessed with a great figure, or even better, a wonderful metabolism. For those of us who were not, we *must* work out. Not only will you *look* good, you will *feel* good because of all the health benefits associated with exercise. Whether you walk, run, play tennis, or lift weights—just do it. You will keep him much more interested in *you*. A healthy lifestyle—including exercise— will help you live longer. We have a responsibility to ourselves to stay healthy.

29.

TWENTY-NINE

Look pretty for him.

A friend of mine once said, "If the barn needs painting, paint it." If your face needs make-up, wear it.

30.

THIRTY

If your husband is a golfer (or tennis player), then go with him to the golf course (or tennis court). Hey, it's a blast watching him hit those little white golf balls and squinting until you can't see them. And see how hard he can swing his racquet! Once in awhile, he would like this sort of hero worship.

31.

THRITY-ONE

If you know he is broke—and you aren't—put
a little cash in his wallet without him knowing.
He will wonder all day long where it came from.

It's so fun for me to tease Ron sometimes when I have a little
WAM (walking around money) and he doesn't. I love to share
anyway, but it seems he is always out of money. I can usually find
loose bills scattered in my purse. (He thinks I take his.) Have a
little mercy, ladies, and loan him some money. You could have even
more fun outlining the rules for paying you back.

32.

THRITY-TWO

Mail a friendship card to him at work—
just a "glad we're together" or "I love you
in so many ways" message.

Hint: Be careful how you address it.
Embarrassing him is not the objective. Stay away
from names like Sweetie Pie, Angel, or Lover Boy.

These friendship cards are easy to find at most drugstores or
supermarkets. It's the element of surprise that makes this work. If
things have been tough for him lately in some way, make the most
of good timing.

33.
THIRTY-THREE

Make sure you pay more attention
to him than you do the family dogs or pets.
(Whatever you do, *don't* confuse their names.)

34.
THIRTY-FOUR

If your husband has a job that keeps him on his
feet all day, surprise him when he gets home with
a hot prepared "foot bath." (You could put on the
new CD you just purchased to help relax him.)

35.

THIRTY-FIVE

If you have your husband's children from a previous marriage, by all means love them as you would your own. This is a huge statement to him about the quality of the woman he found in you. Stepchildren can always use another positive influence in their lives. Make sure *you* are one!

Her children arise up, and call her blessed.
Proverbs 31:28

If you have your own children as well as his, don't show favoritism. They are *all* yours now and need the same love and affection. No one can replace their own mother, but you can learn to be a friend. It's not always easy, but he will love you all the more for loving his children.

36.

Get a life! The best thing any woman can do
for herself and her husband is to develop her
own interests. Get involved in worthwhile causes—
church work, children's issues, community volunteer
work, or the like. Be interesting, have something
to say. Offering your time and energy creates a
sense of value that will do wonders for your own
self-esteem—raising your stock in his eyes too.

Who can find a virtuous woman?
Proverbs 31:10

37.
THIRTY-SEVEN

Get up extra early every once in a while
to make him his favorite breakfast.

There is nothing like the smell of a home-cooked breakfast. Neither one of us has much time, but on some Saturdays, I like to make him homemade biscuits with gravy, scrambled eggs, and bacon. He seems satisfied all day long. Take time to make your husband his favorites.

38.
THIRTY-EIGHT

Do anything and everything to show him you are
his best friend. Listen to him, talk to him,
understand what makes him tick, and respond
to him with compassion and understanding.

She openeth her mouth with wisdom;
and in her tongue is the law of kindness.
Proverbs 31:26

39.

When he makes a mistake, tell him it is okay.
Never fuss and criticize. You will only drive
him away. You are responsible for YOUR
actions and reactions, so make sure they are
loving, compassionate, and understanding.

*Because thou shalt forget thy misery, and
remember it as waters that pass away.*
Job 11:16

Face it: He is going to make mistakes—burn clothes with the
iron, forget to take the cake out of the oven when you asked him to
watch it, spill paint on the carpet. It happens. He doesn't need to
hear about it from you in one of those irritating tones. In the long
run, none of these things really matter.

40.
FORTY

Learn to whisper sweet nothings
in his ear or sweet somethings.

(You never know what this could lead to.)

Don't take this lightly. If you don't know what kind of "nothings" your husband likes, you could have fun experimenting. This tip is not just for at home; it can be done anywhere. Learn how to be the twinkle in his eye. Practice saying thoughtful or romantic things to him—at home, in the car, out on date night, or even at the ball game. Maybe he'll take you home early!

41.

FORTY-ONE

Wake him one morning with a gentle massage.

Hint: He may not want to get
out of bed, so be sure to start early.

Once I'm up and have gotten a start on things, I like to gently massage Ron around his neck or back and help wake him. I know, you're thinking I'm going overboard. Don't worry. I always remind him about how good he's got it, and how lucky he is.

42.
FORTY-TWO

If you can get away with it, call his boss one day and ask for permission to have an extended lunch hour to spend more time with your husband.

43.
FORTY-THREE

Take time for date night and your relationship. Go to a movie or a quiet dinner at your favorite spot. It is very important to keep romance alive.

44.

FORTY-FOUR

Pack his bags and surprise him with
a weekend getaway. You pick the place
and work everything out in advance.

I know that this is sometimes hard to do, but it can be done.
You don't have to go someplace exotic; maybe just plan a weekend
away at a hotel in a nearby city. This is great stress management for
both of you. If you can afford a trip, I promise you will have a
memorable time. Be bold, be daring, and be different.

45.

FORTY-FIVE

Brag on your husband to your friends.
Too many women bash men. If you praise
your man, other people will notice. It is refreshing
to hear about a happily married couple. Be a
good example and encourage other wives.

Her husband is known in the gates,
when he sitteth among the elders of the land.
Proverbs 31:23

When you are really in love with someone, it should show. I find myself talking to my friends about all the wonderful things my husband is to me. They are always asking me if he has a brother. Ron and I both talk to others about each other. It's very obvious that we are in love, and that is how it should be. Your praise will help to bring out the best in him.

46.

FORTY-SIX

Tell him often that you just
keep falling in love with him.

47.

FORTY-SEVEN

Don't play guessing games with your husband.
He'll never figure you out anyway. I always make
it easy for mine. I told him right up front that
I came with a set of "easy to use" instructions.
Just tell him what you need, and it will drastically
reduce frustration and blood pressure levels.

48.

FORTY-EIGHT

Give him lots of space if he needs it.

Sometimes we all need some space.

We wives shouldn't be threatened by

our husbands' needing some time alone.

Don't cling. If he needs to get out of the house for a while to hunt, play golf, or hang out with his friends, let him go without words or your opinions. He needs time away from you too. If you are being the kind of wife you should be, it's not likely he will stay gone too long.

49.

Take his car for an oil change sometime.
If he usually does this, reverse the roles and
you do it. He will be so happy that you
took the time to take care of this.

Hint: Try to find out what kind of oil he's been using. Be
sure you use the same kind, or this little tip could backfire.
Try to go to the same place he does to change the oil.
If you can't remember what kind of oil, look for that little
sticker they put on his car the last time it was changed.

46

50.
FIFTY

If your husband has a bad habit,
do all you can to help him change it.

I can do all things through Christ which strengtheneth me.
Philippians 4:13

First of all, ask him in a very sweet tone of voice if he is aware that he has a bad habit that is *not* good for him. (You have to get him to see it first.) Then, assure him you are going to help support him through the process of changing that habit. Start by gently reminding him that breaking the habit will make him feel good about himself. Habits are the result of simple choices, and by making a *new* simple choice, he can reverse the process. They say it takes twenty-one days to break a habit, so the new choice has to be made over and over. Make sure you offer a great reward for his success.

51.
FIFTY-ONE

If you are traveling somewhere and are lost,
please don't make him ask for directions.
He will eventually find it. Just be patient!

*Yea, though I walk through the valley of
the shadow of death, I will fear no evil.*
Psalm 23:4

This is a guy thing. Why do they hate to ask for directions? Men would rather run out of gas looking for some place than to stop to ask for help. I usually call ahead and ask for directions, so I've got them written down. Then, as we are on the way, I can "suggest" we go this way or that.

52.
FIFTY-TWO

Help him find and match all of his socks.
(They disappear in our home—is this universal?)

53.
FIFTY-THREE

Brag on him to *his* parents! Tell them what a
great job they did raising their son. Parents always
love to hear this, and it endears you to them.

Thy wife shall be as a fruitful vine by the sides of thine house.
Psalm 128:3

54.

FIFTY-FOUR

Fill his car with gas. Have it washed for him, too.

Hint: This is a good time to leave
one of those little love notes in his car.

55.

FIFTY-FIVE

Ask your hubby if he would like to become a
"secret shopper" and invite him to a lingerie shop.
He might surprise you and come along—or you
can give him a private fashion show at home.

56.
FIFTY-SIX

If you buy something that needs
to be put together, hire someone
else to put it together. Please.

Whether it's for your children, or something for you, do
yourself a *big* favor—buy it assembled. It seems like every time we
get a simple project with "easy-to-assemble" instructions, or "no
tools necessary," it takes us until 2:00 in the morning to finish,
especially on Christmas Eve. Hire the elves!

57.

FIFTY-SEVEN

Be his caretaker. Help look after him. He probably
needs you to help him keep up with all of his stuff.

Be discreet and sensitive to that male ego.

He doesn't have to know what you are up to.

It's sometimes just the small things that make such a difference
to him. Once I bought Ron two extra pairs of sunglasses and three
extra sets of car keys. These are things he has a problem finding, so
it made his life so much easier. Find ways to lighten his load.

58.
FIFTY-EIGHT

Make sure he knows you think he is your Prince Charming! (So maybe he doesn't have a white horse. Does he have a white car, perhaps?)

59.
FIFTY-NINE

Learn to be a faithful friend and a faithful servant. Be so awesome that he couldn't replace you with ten women. Why would he want to? (My husband stops strangers on the street to say, "Ask me about my wife!")

60.
SIXTY

If your husband wants to spend time with some of his "buddies," let him go. In fact, bake them a batch of your wonderful chocolate chip cookies. The other guys will be so envious because you are so good to your husband.

She is like the merchants' ships; she bringeth her food from afar.
Proverbs 31:14

61.

Use your creative, imaginative side as
often as you can. You know—lights out,
candles lit, kids asleep—the rest is up to you.

*Let her be as the loving hind and pleasant roe; let her breasts
satisfy thee at all times; and be thou ravished always with her love.*
Proverbs 5:19

With just a little imagination, you can have him eating out of
the palm of your hand. You can also get just about anything you want.
I'll bet he will help you do anything you need at this point. Besides,
intimacy is such a wonderful thing, and it is good for *both* of you.

62.
SIXTY-TWO

If your husband is worried about something,
pray with him about it. Stay by his side,
reminding him that he can count on
you—and God—to be there for him.

*All things, whatsoever ye shall ask
in prayer, believing, ye shall receive.*
Matthew 21:22

There will always be situations that arise to shake us: loss of
a loved one, job troubles, or a challenging financial situation. Whatever it is, the most powerful thing you can do is to seek God's face
and pray. Let your husband know you are praying about it, and
even pray with him.

63.

If he likes to hunt or fish, ask him if you
can go along on the next trip with him.

Hint: If he says yes and you go, don't start talking about how
cute the little deer is when he is about to shoot. I don't believe he'd
ever let you go again.

He that handleth a matter wisely shall find good.
Proverbs 16:20

64.
SIXTY-FOUR

Tell him if you could do it all over again,

you would choose him and marry him again.

This probably has its best effect after you have been married a few years. After all you and your husband have been through, he may wonder if you think it has been worth it. Of course, if you love him, you will say, "Absolutely!" Make sure he knows in every way that you would say "yes" all over again.

65.
SIXTY-FIVE

When it comes to the finances in

your home, try to let him lead the way.

If you feel he needs help, call a professional.

Hint: The last thing you need here, girls, is to be a part of the problem. Quick! Get rid of that new credit card you just applied for.

66.

SIXTY-SIX

Show up at his office one day looking

your absolute best. Sit back and watch

him spread his feathers like a peacock.

It's a universal male thing: showing off his woman.

This is one of those male ego things, but if the occasion is right, let him gloat. It never hurts to raise his stock in the eyes of others by showing up at his office looking like "dynamite." Now if you happen to bring a plate of chocolate chip cookies, you will really score big.

67.
SIXTY-SEVEN

Notice little things for him such as
his shoes, ties, or suits. If it's time for new ones,
make sure he gets them. He may just need
you to sew a few buttons on his shirts. Do it!
He will just love knowing you notice—and care.

The LORD God said, It is not good that the man should be alone;
I will make him an help meet for him.
Genesis 2:18

68.
SIXTY-EIGHT

If golf is his game, surprise him by arranging

for him to have a private lesson, or two.

Or if he's into fitness, hire a personal

trainer for a couple of consultations.

69.
SIXTY-NINE

If you have a special remodeling job for him
to do at home, tell him you will be
glad to help. Don't worry, as remodeling
often goes, it will probably be the last time
you will work together on such a project.

Hint: You should count on breaking
a nail or two, so don't panic.

70.

SEVENTY

Make his birthday a month-long celebration.

It's called the birthday month! Show him

that he is worth celebrating.

All month long you can go out of your way to do special things for him: a special dinner that he likes you to make or maybe a certain thing he likes to do. Give in and spoil him the entire month. Maybe he will reciprocate when it's *your* birthday.

71.

SEVENTY-ONE

Encourage your husband in his job. If he dislikes what he is doing, support him in finding another job. If he likes his job, let him enjoy talking about it to you. When he knows you support him, he will be much more successful.

72.

Go with him to run errands on the weekend.
Be together as much as possible. Find reasons to
be together even if it's a trip to the hardware store.

Every wise woman buildeth her house.
Proverbs 14:1

This is easy for me because we are so inseparable. I love to be with Ron no matter what we are doing. We run errands together, like taking clothes to the cleaners, buying stamps at the post office, or maybe picking up a few things at the grocery store. Sometimes we run errands together that seem totally insignificant, but we *are* together, and that's what we love. Go with him, ladies, if just for the company.

73.

SEVENTY-THREE

Surprise him sometime and have the yard work
done before he gets home. (If you can't start
the mower, hire the local kids.) It will be
a win-win for all. He will be so appreciative.

74.

SEVENTY-FOUR

If you are together when the local radio station is playing
that "special song," stop what you are doing and go get
him to listen with you and share a special remembrance
together. (If I hear our song, and my husband isn't there,
I call him and play it through the phone as soon
as he picks up. It always says "I love you" to him.)

75.

SEVENTY-FIVE

If you are out and about somewhere, and you see your "old flame," better just blow it out!

It never fails. When I go places with my husband, these former boyfriends appear. When I go places with my husband, we run into former boyfriends of mine. But it doesn't phase him in the least because he knows I chose him. But I did marry Ron in 1992. I said I would never marry until I met a man I couldn't live without. Reassure your husband that he was your ultimate choice.

76.
SEVENTY-SIX

Go to the local park sometime for a simple,
romantic lunch. Take a book of romantic poetry
or "great thoughts" and read it to him. Share some
inspiring words with him. Romantic words and
inspiring thoughts can trigger some great new ideas.

77.
SEVENTY-SEVEN

Surprise him: *don't* invite
your mother for the weekend.

78.

SEVENTY-EIGHT

Clip coupons! Be frugal.

A virtuous woman is a crown to her husband.
Proverbs 12:4

79.

SEVENTY-NINE

Start making a list of all the qualities you love about your husband. A big list. Then, make a reservation at your favorite restaurant. Over dinner, share the big list with him.

Hint: I recommend that you keep this list with you at all times. There may come a time when you need to refresh your *own* memory.

80.
EIGHTY

If you cannot afford to buy him a diamond, *be* one.

*Delight thyself also in the LORD; and
he shall give thee the desires of thine heart.*
Psalm 37:4

The recurring theme I wish to get across in this book is not just to look for things that you can do for your husband, but rather to be totally aware of your attitude in all things. When you truly love him, you will want to find ways to express your love and feelings. It becomes a by-product of deep love and devotion. You will look for ways to show him more love.

81.

EIGHTY-ONE

Drop whatever you are doing if he needs you for anything. Sometimes—even if they won't admit it—our husbands *need* us. You can help by giving your husband a boost, an encouraging word, or a touch. At the very least, just be there for him.

Iron sharpeneth iron; so a man
sharpeneth the countenance of his friend.
Proverbs 27:17

82.
EIGHTY-TWO

Never go to bed at night with negative
feelings or unresolved issues between you.
(It won't be any better by morning.)

Let not the sun go down upon your wrath.
Ephesians 4:26

This is very important. Whatever squabbles you've had before going to bed, they will not go away overnight. Learn to resolve any conflict between the two of you. If you don't, it will fester and not end well. Put away your conflict, talk things out, and make up. Then enjoy a good night's sleep.

83.

EIGHTY-THREE

Save money. Plan your financial future together.

Riches and honour are with me:
yea, durable riches and righteousness.
Proverbs 8:18

I must admit that I'm not too good at this. There are just too many things I haven't experienced, and they all cost money. Ron says if I want to experience anything later down the road, then I'd better help "put away" and not "take away." Help each other save money. If he's a better saver than you are, don't undo his hard work.

84.
EIGHTY-FOUR

If your husband suddenly notices he's been losing
his hair, don't recommend transplant surgery
or hair growing products. It will only make him
more sensitive about it. Just love him as he is.

"Even the very hairs of your head are all numbered."
Matthew 10:30 NIV

85.

EIGHTY-FIVE

When he gets sick and has to stay in bed,

be there at his side as much as possible.

Let him hear you whisper a prayer for him.

Is any among you afflicted? let him pray.
Is any merry? let him sing psalms.
James 5:13

86.
EIGHTY-SIX

If you are not a good cook, take lessons!

It's true: the way to a man's heart

is through his stomach.

87.
EIGHTY-SEVEN

Keep the house clean and organized. This will
help everyone, including you. (It also gives you
a great excuse to go to the container store!)

My husband is the neat freak in the family, so nothing makes
him happier than to walk into a clean, picked-up, organized,
smooth-running house. I love to be clean; it's just that I scatter
things here and there like a kid. When asked where something
belongs my usual reply is, "Wherever you put it, that's where it goes."
If it makes him happy, gals, do it yourself—or sneak in a maid.

88.

EIGHTY-EIGHT

Keep a current picture of your husband
in your wallet. It is one of those things
he will delight in knowing you do.
(Just make sure *he* thinks it's a flattering picture.)

89.

EIGHTY-NINE

Compliment your husband on the small things
he does. Praise goes such a long way. Learn this,
and you can accomplish almost anything with him.

His praise shall continually be in my mouth.
Psalm 34:1

90.
NINETY

If your husband feels he is losing his "competitive edge" in life and he's down about getting older, find as many ways as possible, and as often as possible, to say kind things to cheer him up.

A word fitly spoken is like apples of gold in pictures of silver.
Proverbs 25:11

91.
NINETY-ONE

Do him a *big* favor: Don't make him put up
Christmas lights this year. If he doesn't want
any more lights, let him off the hook for once.

Every year my vision for more lights grows. Putting those things
up reminds me of Chevy Chase in the movie *Christmas Vacation*. Poor
Ron . . . every time he thinks he's got it right, three more fuses blow,
the reindeer fall down, and only half the tree is lit. He no longer
wants a tree or decorations. In fact, he's ready to skip Christmas
altogether. Go easy on him with the decor if at all possible.

92.
NINETY-TWO

If he carries a pager, devise a secret code
you can send him during the day that says,
"I love you" or "I'm thinking about you."
I guarantee he will smile wherever he is.

Commit thy works unto the LORD,
and thy thoughts shall be established.
Proverbs 16:3

We have had so much fun through the years, even when we couldn't be together. We would devise certain numbers to get across a message. When we didn't have cell phones, this came in handy, especially when one of us was on the road. Try this with your husband. You can always be in touch.

93.
NINETY-THREE

Spend time making and discussing future plans with your husband. These things build and promote security for both of you, and it says you plan to be together "til death do us part."

God is my strength and power: and he maketh my way perfect.
2 Samuel 22:33

94.

NIENTY-FOUR

Be his biggest fan and his loudest cheerleader
when he accomplishes something significant in
his life. Share in the moments that excite him.
Let him know how proud you are of him.

Hint: This is not rocket science, you know.
I brag on my husband just for keeping our
cars clean. These days, that is no small feat.

95.

NINETY-FIVE

Reorganize his closet for him sometime.
Maybe you will find something he's been
looking for and something you forgot you had—
all because you sorted the stuff in his closet.
Who knows what treasures will turn up!

Sometimes I can't even keep my own closet organized, but I do
like to help. When I'm going through his closet, I usually take a few
of his long-sleeved shirts for winter that I like to lounge around in.
He thinks they are just disappearing. Hey, you might find a whole
new wardrobe in there! You may also find other interesting articles
that belong in the kids' toy box or even the garage.

96.
NINETY-SIX

Take time to visit one of your old favorite hangouts. Just go sit and reminisce about simpler times in your life. Reflecting on where we've traveled from and what has brought us to where we are today encourages us. We can see how the hand of God has guided our lives. This builds faith.

This will mean more to you as the years go by. We often visit favorite old places in the town we live in and other places, too. Do this often. Look back and see how God has walked with you, guiding your moves.

97.
NINETY-SEVEN

Run the kids to the little league games for him sometime and let him stay at home. This gives him the "day off." Some of these transporting errands just wear you out, don't they?

98.

Buy his favorite cologne one day,
telling him you want him to smell good
enough to eat! Believe me, he'll wear it.

Have you ever purchased your husband's favorite cologne? I
buy what I like him to wear. If your husband likes to wear cologne,
get him some. If he doesn't wear it, encourage him to. Let him
know what it does to you, and he'll wear it.

99.

NINETY-NINE

Always be a great example to him, as well as to others, of what a godly, virtuous woman should be. Never behave in such a way that you have to apologize for yourself.

The wisdom that is from above is first pure, then peaceable, gentle, and easy to be intreated, full of mercy and good fruits, without partiality, and without hypocrisy.
James 3:17

Casting all your care on him; for he careth for you.
1 Peter 5:7

My yoke is easy, and my burden is light.
Matthew 11:30

Make a joyful noise unto the LORD.
Psalm 100:1

100.
ONE HUNDRED

Be fun! Hey ladies—lighten up!

The emphasis is on *fun!* Too many of us walk around like we are sucking on lemons. Who in the world wants to be around someone like that? Our lives should be a reflection of God, who created us and this world in which we live.

We, as wives, can set an example and help create an environment in our homes that makes it easy to be around us, as well as fun.

101.

ONE HUNDRED ONE

Live each day to the fullest, making it count.
Living this way will help you to live and
grow to be an incredible, fulfilled woman.

Ladies, when you do the things I have suggested, your husband will follow you to the ends of the earth. After all, isn't that what we all want—a long, lasting, satisfying relationship with the man of our dreams?

Make every day count. When you practice living a joy-filled life, giving to and serving others, you are pleasing to God. And your husband will be a new man. Learn and practice enjoying the simple things in life. When, in the end, you have walked hand in hand with your husband through the roads of life and you truly love each other, you will find you have *everything* you need.

A special "thank you" to my mother, "Baby Jean."

It was you who molded me into the woman I am today. Thank you for taking your role seriously as a woman, wife, and mother. Your endless love, devotion, and guidance have been a source of strength and comfort for me.

You and Dad sacrificed for your children and gave us a foundation of love. I'm forever thankful for a mother and father who loved each other, gave to each other, and supported one another with their respective roles and duties, regardless of how challenging it might have been. Thank you for never quitting! By your example, you taught me how to serve others and give unselfishly. Thank you for your servanthood and wisdom.

Thank you, Mom, most of all, for the way you spoiled and loved my daddy before he passed away. What a blessing it is for me today to live knowing you took such good care of him, showing me what unconditional love is all about. I know my husband thanks you.

You're one terrific mom. I love you!—Tena

ABOUT THE AUTHOR

Tena Brown has been married to Ron since 1992. Ron describes her as "more than I could ever dream of," saying she takes good care of him, spoils him totally, and is "irreplaceable."

Tena is stepmother to Ron's two teenaged sons, who authored the book *101 Ways to Spoil Your Parents*. She is also the mother of two *perfect* poodles. Tena is founder and president of a marketing company that promotes specialty hotels overseas. She is a personal coach for professionals, focusing her attention on adversity coaching and life skills. She was the personal coach to the Longhorn football team at the University of Texas during the 1990 and 1991 seasons, teaching the "mental art of winning at football and at life—on and off the field." She is a frequent public speaker for several community, religious, and professional organizations.

Tena attended the University of Oklahoma and earned a bachelor's of business administration from East Central University in Ada, Oklahoma.

The Browns make their home in Arlington, Texas.

If you would like to contact the author, you may write to her at this e-mail address: 101ways@home.com

Additional copies of this book
are available from your local bookstore.

Also available from Honor Books:
101 Ways to Spoil Your Wife
by Ron Brown

If you have enjoyed this book, or if it has
impacted your life, we would like to hear from you.

Please contact us at:
Honor Books
Department E
P.O. Box 55388
Tulsa, Oklahoma 74155

Or by e-mail at *info@honorbooks.com*

Tulsa, Oklahoma